'No guest is so welcome
in a friend's house
that he will not
become a nuisance
after three days.'

Titus Maccius Plautus

ROMAN COOKERY

Recipes & History

by
Jane Renfrew

with a Foreword by
Loyd Grossman OBE

ENGLISH HERITAGE

Front cover: Detail from a Roman mosaic pavement, 1st or 2nd century

Endpapers: Animals used for food depicted on Romano-British objects. *Top left:* Bull's head bucket-handle mount, Felmersham on Ouse, Bedfordshire; *Top right:* Bronze figure of a boar, Hounslow, London; *Centre:* Hare brooch, Lincoln; *Bottom left:* Cockerel brooch, Brough Castle, Cumbria; *Bottom right:* Bronze figure of a roped stag, Milber Down Fort, Devon

Published by English Heritage, 23 Savile Row, London W1S 2ET

Copyright © English Heritage and Jane Renfrew
First published 1985
Revised edition 2004

ISBN 1 85074 870 5

Product code 50851

Edited by Susan Kelleher, Publishing, English Heritage, Kemble Drive, Swindon SN2 2GZ
Designed by Pauline Hull
Picture research by Elaine Willis
Brought to press by Andrew McLaren
Printed in England by CPI Bath

CONTENTS

FOREWORD

Would the pyramids have been built without the recently invented bread to efficiently feed the workforce? Food is a common denominator between us all, and a potent link with our ancestors, just as much as an ancient parish church or a listed house.

I am delighted to contribute a Foreword to English Heritage's series of historic cookery books, which neatly combine two of my passions – history and food. Most of us no longer have to catch or grow our own food before eating it, but the continuing daily need for sustenance still powerfully links us with our earliest forebears. We may not like the thought of Roman fish sauce made from fermented entrails (until we next add oyster sauce to a Chinese beef dish), but we can only sigh with recognition at a Jacobean wife's exhortation to 'let yor butter bee scalding hott in yor pan' before pouring in the beaten eggs for an omelette. The Roman penchant for dormice cooked in milk doesn't resonate with us now, but a dish of pears in red wine features at modern dinner parties just as it did in medieval times.

Food and cooking have inevitably changed down the centuries, as modern cookers have supplanted open hearths, and increased wealth and speedy transport have opened up modern tastes and palates to the widest range of ingredients and cuisines. But it's worth remembering that it was the Romans who gave us onions, sugar was an expensive luxury in the 16th century as was tea in the 17th, the tomato only became popular in Europe in the 19th century and even in the 1950s avocados and red peppers were still exotic foreign imports.

I urge you to experiment with the recipes in these books which cover over 2,000 years, and hope you enjoy, as I have, all that is sometimes strange and often familiar about the taste of times past.

Loyd Grossman OBE
Former Commissioner of English Heritage
Chairman of the Campaign for Museums

INTRODUCTION

When the Roman legions invaded Britain in AD 43 they heralded many changes for these islands and, by bringing us into the Roman Empire, they gave us access to a new world of sophisticated tastes. These were apparent in many spheres but not least in agriculture, foods and cooking.

In reconstructing the diet of Roman Britain there are several sources of evidence to draw on. Firstly, there is the physical evidence of the bones and seeds recovered during excavations. Then there is the literary evidence which comes in two forms: the letters preserved by Vindolanda, written by soldiers serving on Hadrian's Wall to their families, where they list their foods as in one case 'spice, goats' milk, salt, young pig, ham, corn, venison and flour'; in another letter, vintage wine, Celtic beer, ordinary wine, fish sauce and pork fat are mentioned. The other literary evidence is of a more general kind: the cookery book of Apicius, the agricultural treatises of Cato, Varro, Columella and Palladius, Pliny's great work on Natural History and the descriptions of notable feasts

Opposite: A selection of butcher's knives of the type used in Roman Britain

> 'Except the vine, there is no plant
> which bears a fruit of as great
> importance as the olive.'
>
> Pliny the Elder (AD 23–79)

such as Trimalchio's feast as described by Petronius. Finally, there are illustrations of foods and dining scenes both in wall paintings and on mosaic, and hunting and vintage scenes depicted on pottery.

The Romans were responsible for the import into Britain of a number of sources of food. The game introduced included pheasants, peacocks, guinea fowl and fallow deer. They also brought many fruit and nut-bearing trees into cultivation and a wide range of herbs and plants which they used in cooking.

Besides introducing animals and crops for rearing and growing in this country, the Romans also imported a number of commodities which they valued in their diet including dates, wine, olive oil, pepper and fermented fish sauce.

The Romans had a profound influence on the development of civilisation, and although not all the new ways were adopted by the indigenous population, a great many of their sophisticated systems of doing things continued to be copied for centuries. In the case of cooking and cuisine they introduced many items into the diet which are still common today, together with methods of cooking

A market stall depicted in a 2nd-century stone relief from Rome's port city of Ostia. The lady stall-holder tempts customers with her selection of live produce as well as a pair of monkeys to provide entertainment. Note the baskets full of live snails, and the heads of the chickens and rabbits poking out from their cages beneath the stall

with which we are very familiar. Undoubtedly the main difference between Roman cooking and that of today was that they had an extraordinary fondness for using a sauce made from the fermented entrails of fish which was used equally often in sweet as in savoury dishes, often combined with liberal amounts of pepper. They also used large amounts of honey in their cooking, and were fond of a wide variety of herbs to flavour their dishes. In their more elaborate feasts great store was set by making dishes look as if they were made from other ingredients – playing a sort of identification game with the guests.

The recipes in this book are based on those of Apicius, whose cookery book is the only one to have come down to us from Roman times. M Gaius Apicius lived at the time of Tiberius, in the 1st century, and apparently wrote two books on cooking: a recipe book and a book on sauces. It appears that the manuscripts which have survived are those of a late 4th-century or early 5th-century edition which also includes extracts from a Greek cookery book of the Imperial period. The recipes which follow are ones that it is more or less practical to try out today and which give an idea of the tastes of the Romans and of their culinary skills. Apicius is rather cavalier with his cooking instructions and so fuller details of quantities, cooking times, and procedures based on contemporary practice have been given. However, each cook must feel free to vary the quantities, especially of herbs, spices and flavourings according to their own personal preferences and experience.

Evidence of the type of foodstuffs enjoyed by the Romans depicted on a fresco in the Villa di Guila Felice in Pompeii

ROMAN BRITAIN – KEY DATES

AD 43 Claudius's invasion of Britain. Roman troops land in Kent at Richborough, Dover and Lympne

60–1 Revolt of Boudicca and the Iceni. Camolodunum (Colchester) sacked and burnt, then Londinium (London) and Verulamium (St Albans) captured before rebellion put down

70–84 Conquest of Wales and the North

78–84 Agricola governor of Britain

Roman coin found in Britain showing the head of Emperor Trajan (AD 98–117)

90–120 Establishment of London as capital of Britannia, and various regional *civitas* capitals

122–8 Construction of Hadrian's Wall from the Tyne to the Solway

c.143 Construction of Antonine Wall along Forth–Clyde line

154 Antonine Wall evacuated due to trouble in the North

192 Death of Emperor Commodus. Succession disputed but won by Septimius Severus

208 Severus and family in Britain Rebuilding of Hadrian's Wall by Severus

211 Death of Severus at York

View along Hadrian's Wall

Many units on Hadrian's Wall
had a symbol. The boar was the
emblem of the Twentieth Legion

Recreating the days of the Roman occupation of Britain

Recipes

A number of standard Roman ingredients need explanation.

Liquamen: Made from the fermented entrails of fish. Anchovy essence in its diluted form, or soy sauce, may be used as a substitute.

Defructum: A cooking wine which has been reduced to at least half its volume by boiling down before use to give a thick consistency.

Caroenum: A very sweet wine, reduced by boiling to a third of its volume and mixed with honey.

Passum: A sweeter wine. A sweet Spanish wine can be used instead.

Mulsum: A mixture of honey and wine which was used as a drink to accompany the first course of a meal.

Amulum: A type of wheat starch for which cornflour is an excellent substitute.

Asafoetida: Available from chemists, but only use very sparingly as just the tiniest drop is needed to give flavour.

PRAWN RISSOLES

24 cooked shelled prawns
a pinch of pepper
5 ml (1 tsp) anchovy essence
1 egg, beaten
flour

Pound the prawns in a mortar with
the pepper and anchovy essence. Mix
in the beaten egg to bind and form
into rissoles. Roll in flour and fry
gently in oil until lightly browned on
both sides.

OYSTERS

3–4 oysters per person
a pinch of pepper
a pinch of ground lovage
2 egg yolks
15 ml (1 tbls) vinegar
15 ml (1 tbls) olive oil
15 ml (1 tbls) wine
5 ml (1 tsp) anchovy essence
15 ml (1 tbls) honey (optional)

Ask your fishmonger to open the oyster
shells, as near as possible to the time of
eating. They can then be served raw or
stewed or baked, covered with the
following sauce. Mix the pepper and
lovage with the egg yolks, then add
the vinegar, a drop at a time, to make a
smooth mixture. Stir in the olive oil, wine,
anchovy essence and honey if using. Mix
all thoroughly together, pour over the
oysters and serve.

MUSSELS WITH LENTILS

575–750 ml (1–1½ pt) mussels
   per person
350 g (12 oz) lentils
1 onion, chopped
a pinch of each of the following:
   peppercorns, cumin seeds,
   coriander seeds, dried mint,
   rue, pennyroyal
15 ml (1 tbls) vinegar
15 ml (1 tbls) honey
15 ml (1 tbls) *defructum*
5 ml (1 tsp) anchovy essence

To serve:
olive oil

Clean the mussels thoroughly, discarding any that are open. Place in a rinsed, wide pan and cover closely with a folded, damp tea-towel. Heat quickly, shaking the pan at intervals, for about 5–7 minutes until the shells are open. Take the mussels from their shells, removing the beards. Pound in a mortar. Put the lentils in a pan of cold water with the onion and bring to the boil. Cook until the lentils are soft. Pound the pepper, cumin, coriander, mint, rue and pennyroyal in a mortar, then mix in the vinegar, honey, *defructum* and anchovy essence, and put into the pan with the lentils. Add the mussels to the lentils, and bring them to the boil, stirring. Serve hot, sprinkled with a few drops of best olive oil.

BOILED MUSSELS

575–750 ml (1–1 1/2 pt) mussels
  per person
a pinch of each of the following:
  celery seeds, rue, peppercorns
15 ml (1 tbls) honey
15 ml (1 tbls) *passum*
15 ml (1 tbls) olive oil
5 ml (1 tsp) anchovy essence
15 ml (1 tbls) cornflour

Prepare and cook the mussels as in
the previous recipe. Remove from
their shells and keep warm. Pound the
celery seeds, rue, pepper and honey
together in a mortar. Add *passum*,
olive oil and anchovy essence, and put
in a pan. Blend in the cornflour and
bring to the boil stirring all the time,
until the sauce thickens. Pour over the
mussels, sprinkle with pepper and
serve.

FISH COOKED IN ITS OWN JUICE

1 salmon, salmon trout or
  ordinary trout
15 ml (1 tbls) salt
15 ml (1 tbls) coriander seeds
15 ml (1 tbls) vinegar

Clean, wash and dry the fish. Pound
the salt and the coriander seeds in a
mortar. Roll the fish in this mixture.
Place the fish in an ovenproof frying
pan, seal by frying quickly on both sides,
then cover with a lid. Put the pan in
the oven and bake at gas mark 4,
180°C (350°F) until the fish is cooked
through. When it is cooked, remove
from the oven, sprinkle with strong
vinegar and serve.

PATINA OF FILLETS OF HAKE

1 hake fillet per person
100 g (4 oz) shelled pine kernels
2 leeks, chopped
2 sticks of celery, chopped
450 g (1 lb) spinach, cooked to a purée
225 g (8 oz) cooked chicken breast, sliced
100 g (4 oz) salami, sliced
4 eggs, hard-boiled and halved
225 g (8 oz) pork sausages, cooked and chopped
3 oysters per person, shelled (or 1 can smoked oysters in oil)
50 g (2 oz) cheese, grated
25 g (1 oz) peppercorns
275 ml (½ pt) milk
a pinch of each of the following: pepper, lovage, celery seeds
1 drop *asafoetida* essence
2 eggs, beaten

To garnish:
sea urchins (optional)

Soak the pine kernels, and let them dry. Fry the hake fillets. Take a shallow ovenproof dish and layer in it the leeks, celery, spinach purée, chicken, salami, hard-boiled eggs, sausages, oysters and cheese. Sprinkle the pine kernels and peppercorns over the top. Put the milk in a saucepan. Add the pepper, lovage and celery seeds, and bring to the boil. Add the *asafoetida* essence and remove from the heat. Mix in the beaten eggs, then pour the sauce over the patina and cook in a moderate oven, gas mark 4, 180°C (350°F) until set. Serve, garnished with sea urchins if wished.

SAUCE FOR SEA BREAM

A pinch of each of the following:
   peppercorns, lovage, caraway
   seeds, celery seeds, dried onion
1 drop *asafoetida* essence
15 ml (1 tbls) wine
15 ml (1 tbls) *passum*
15 ml (1 tbls) vinegar
15 ml (1 tbls) olive oil
5 ml (1 tsp) anchovy essence
15 ml (1 tbls) cornflour

Grind together the pepper, lovage, caraway, celery seeds and dried onion. Moisten with *asafoetida* essence and add the wine, *passum*, vinegar, olive oil and anchovy essence. Put the mixture in a saucepan, blend in the cornflour and heat until boiling, stirring all the time. Remove from heat when the sauce has thickened, and serve with sea bream.

SAUCE FOR YOUNG TUNNY FISH

A pinch each of the following:
   pepper, lovage, oregano, fresh
   coriander
1 onion, thinly sliced
50 g (2 oz) stoned raisins
15 ml (1 tbls) *passum*
15 ml (1 tbls) vinegar
15 ml (1 tbls) *defructum*
15 ml (1 tbls) olive oil
5 ml (1 tsp) anchovy essence
honey (optional)

Pound the pepper, herbs, onion and raisins in a mortar. Put in a saucepan with the liquid ingredients, and bring to the boil. Add honey to taste if liked. Serve with grilled or boiled tunny fish.

MILK-FED SNAILS

6 edible snails per person
1 litre (1¾ pt) milk
salt

To serve:
5 ml (1 tsp) anchovy essence
15 ml (1 tbls) wine

Clean the snails with a sponge and remove the membranes so that they can come out of their shells. Put in a vessel with half the milk and salt for 1 day, then in a fresh vessel with the remaining milk for 1 more day, cleaning away the excrement every hour. When the snails are fattened to the point where they cannot return to their shells, fry them in oil. Serve with a dressing of anchovy essence and wine.

MEAT PIECES À LA APICIUS

T-bone beef steaks, or pork chops,
or leg steaks of pork or mutton
a pinch of each of the following:
pepper, lovage, cyperus, cumin
5 ml (1 tsp) anchovy essence
30 ml (2 tbls) *passum*

Bone the meat, roll up the pieces, tie together with string and put in the oven to seal at gas mark 7, 220°C (425°F) for about 10 minutes. Remove from the oven and put under a low grill, taking care not to burn them. Pound the pepper, lovage, cyperus and cumin in a mortar and blend with the anchovy essence and *passum*. Put the meat in a pan with this sauce and simmer gently until completely cooked. Remove the meat from the pan with a slotted spoon and serve without the sauce, sprinkled with pepper.

SUCKING PIG À LA FLACCUS

1 sucking pig
salt
a pinch of each of the following:
  pepper, lovage, caraway seeds,
  celery seeds, rue
1 drop *asafoetida* essence
5 ml (1 tsp) anchovy essence
45 ml (3 tbls) wine
15 ml (1 tbls) *passum*
10 ml (2 tsps) olive oil
15 ml (1 tbls) cornflour

To serve:
ground celery seeds

Clean the pig. Sprinkle with salt and roast at gas mark 4, 180°C (350°F) allowing 25 minutes per 450 g (1 lb) plus 25 minutes. While it is cooking, pound the pepper, lovage, caraway, celery seeds and rue in a mortar. Moisten with *asafoetida* essence and anchovy essence, then blend in the wine and *passum*. Put in a saucepan with the olive oil and bring to the boil. Thicken with cornflour mixed with water. Add the juices from the roast sucking pig, bring to the boil and simmer gently until thickened. Pour over the pig, and sprinkle with ground celery seeds. Serve hot.

Romano-British bronze figure of a boar found at Hounslow, London

HOT LAMB STEW

**700–900g (1½–2 lb) lean loin,
neck or breast of lamb, cubed**
1 small onion, finely chopped
5 ml (1 tsp) coriander seeds
**a pinch of each of the following:
pepper, lovage, cumin**
5 ml (1 tsp) anchovy essence
15 ml (1 tbls) olive oil
15 ml (1 tbls) wine
15 ml (1 tbls) cornflour

Put the pieces of meat into a saucepan and toss in hot oil to seal. Pound the onion, coriander seeds, pepper, lovage and cumin in a mortar. Mix with the anchovy essence, olive oil and wine. Pour this mixture over the meat in the pan and simmer gently for about 2 hours, until tender. Mix the cornflour with a little water and add to the stew to thicken the sauce. Stir until boiling. Serve hot.

24

SAUCE FOR MEAT SLICES

**A pinch of each of the following:
pepper, lovage, caraway seeds,
dried mint, spikenard**
1 egg yolk
15 ml (1 tbls) honey
15 ml (1 tbls) vinegar
15 ml (1 tbls) olive oil
5 ml (1 tsp) anchovy essence
1 bay leaf
1 leek (optional)
15 ml (1 tbls) cornflour

Pound the pepper, lovage, caraway, mint and spikenard in a mortar, then mix together with the egg yolk, honey, vinegar, olive oil and anchovy essence. Place in a pan over a low heat, and add the bay leaf. A leek may also be added for extra flavour if desired. Blend in the cornflour and stir until thickened. Remove leek and bay leaf and pour immediately over the meat slices.

HOT SAUCE FOR ROAST VENISON

225 g (8 oz) dried damsons, soaked overnight
a pinch of each of the following: pepper, lovage, parsley
15 ml (1 tbls) honey
15 ml (1 tbls) wine
15 ml (1 tbls) vinegar
5 ml (1 tsp) anchovy essence
olive oil
1 leek, chopped
1 savory plant

Drain the damsons. Put a drop of olive oil into a pan, add the damsons and all the rest of the ingredients. Cook slowly over a low heat for about 1 hour. Serve with roast venison.

HOT BOILED GOOSE WITH COLD SAUCE

1 goose
a pinch of each of the following: pepper, lovage, coriander seeds, mint, rue
5 ml (1 tsp) anchovy essence
15 ml (1 tbls) olive oil

Place the goose in a large saucepan. Barely cover with cold water and simmer the bird for approximately 2½ hours until tender. Dry with a clean cloth and keep warm. Pound the pepper, lovage, coriander seeds, mint and rue in a mortar. Add the anchovy essence and olive oil, together with the juices from the pan. Pour over the bird and serve.

BOILED PARTRIDGE

1 partridge

a pinch of each of the following:
    pepper, lovage, celery seeds,
    mint, myrtle berries or raisins

15 ml (1 tbls) wine

15 ml (1 tbls) vinegar

15 ml (1 tbls) olive oil

5 ml (1 tsp) anchovy essence

5 ml (1 tsp) honey

Place the partridge with its feathers on in a large saucepan. Cover with cold water and simmer gently for about 45 minutes over a low heat. Pluck the bird when cooled but still wet.

A freshly killed partridge may be plucked first and then braised in the sauce so that it does not get too tough. To make the sauce: pound together the pepper, lovage, celery seeds, mint, myrtle berries or raisins in a mortar, and then mix them with the wine, vinegar, olive oil, anchovy essence and honey. This makes a pleasant cold dressing to serve with the cooled partridge.

A stone carving of a bunch of myrtle found at Wroxeter Roman City in Shropshire

BOILED CHICKEN

I boiling chicken
a pinch of each of the following:
  pepper, cumin, thyme, fennel
  seeds, mint, rue
I drop *asafoetida* essence
30 ml (2 tbls) vinegar
100 g (4 oz) stoned dates
15 ml (I tbls) honey
15 ml (I tbls) olive oil
5 ml (I tsp) anchovy essence

Put the chicken in a saucepan. Cover with water and simmer gently for 2½–3 hours until thoroughly cooked. Dry well. Pound the pepper, cumin, thyme, fennel seeds, mint and rue in a mortar and moisten with a drop of *asafoetida* essence. Add the vinegar and dates and pound until well blended. Stir in the honey, oil and anchovy essence. Pour over the chicken and serve either hot or cold.

SAUCE FOR ROAST WOOD PIGEONS

A pinch of each of the following:
  pepper, lovage, fresh
  coriander, mint, dried onion
100 g (4 oz) stoned dates
I egg yolk
15 ml (I tbls) wine
15 ml (I tbls) vinegar
15 ml (I tbls) olive oil
15 ml (I tbls) honey
5 ml (I tsp) anchovy essence

Pound the pepper, herbs and onion together in a mortar. Add the dates and egg yolk and pound until smooth. Mix the remaining ingredients in a pan, add the mixture from the mortar, and heat gently until the sauce thickens, stirring all the time. Pour over roast pigeons and serve.

STUFFED HARE

1 hare
225 g (8 oz) whole pine kernels
100 g (4 oz) shelled almonds
100 g (4 oz) chopped mixed nuts
25 g (1 oz) peppercorns
2 eggs, beaten
a pinch of each of the following:
   pepper, rue, savory
1 small onion, chopped
100 g (4 oz) stoned dates
5 ml (1 tsp) anchovy essence
30 ml (2 tbls) spiced wine

Mix together the pine kernels, almonds, chopped mixed nuts, peppercorns and add the chopped giblets of the hare. Bind with the eggs and use the mixture to stuff the hare. Wrap the hare in baking foil and roast in the oven at gas mark 5, 190°C (375°F) for 1–1½ hours until tender. To make the sauce: put the pepper, rue, savory, chopped onion, dates, anchovy essence, spiced wine and the juices from the roast hare in a saucepan. Let this boil gently until thickened and serve with the hare.

Romano-British hare brooch found at Lincoln

WHITE MICE IN A GREEN HERB SAUCE
(not real mice!)

6 hard-boiled eggs
12 blanched almonds
chives
cloves or peppercorns

For the sauce:
2.5 ml ('/2 tsp) ground pepper
1 ml ('/4 tsp) cumin
pinch of caraway seeds
small bay leaf
fresh herbs to taste (thyme,
    oregano, lovage, celery leaf)
50 g (2 oz) dates, finely chopped
5 ml (1 tsp) wine vinegar
60 ml (4 tbls) vegetable stock
60 ml (4 tbls) white wine
10 ml (2 tsps) olive oil

Grind the pepper, caraway, cumin and bay leaf together in a mortar. Add the green herbs tied in a muslin bag, finely chopped dates, vinegar, wine, stock and olive oil. Bring to a boil, then simmer gently for 20 minutes to reduce. Remove herb bag. Cut the hard-boiled eggs in half lengthways and place side by side on a serving plate. Place sliced almonds as 'ears', cloves or peppercorns as 'eyes' and use the chives as 'tails'. Pour over the sauce and serve.

Note: Make sure you do not eat the 'eyes'.

SAUCE FOR SOFT-BOILED EGGS

100 g (4 oz) shelled pine kernels
a pinch of pepper
a pinch of lovage
15 ml (1 tbls) honey
15 ml (1 tbls) vinegar

Soak the pine kernels and let them dry. Pound the pepper, lovage and pine kernels in a mortar until smooth. Mix with honey and vinegar, and pour this sauce over freshly boiled eggs which have been removed from their shells.

Romano-British cockerel brooch found at Brough Castle, Cumbria

PEAS À LA VITELLIUS

700 g (1½ lb) dried peas, soaked
overnight
a pinch of each of the following:
pepper, lovage, ginger
yolks of 2 hard-boiled eggs
45 ml (3 tbls) honey
5 ml (1 tsp) anchovy essence
15 ml (1 tbls) wine
15 ml (1 tbls) vinegar
15 ml (1 tbls) olive oil

Boil the peas for about 1½ hours until very soft. Stir to make a smooth mixture. Pound the pepper, lovage and ginger in a mortar and mix with the hard-boiled egg yolks, honey, anchovy essence, wine and vinegar. Put the pounded mixture in a saucepan, add the olive oil and bring to the boil. Add to the peas, stirring until smooth and heated through, then serve.

TRUFFLES

12 large truffles
salt
15 ml (1 tbls) olive oil
5 ml (1 tsp) anchovy essence
15 ml (1 tbls) wine
15 ml (1 tbls) *caroenum*
15 ml (1 tbls) honey
a pinch of pepper
10 ml (2 tsps) cornflour

Scrape the truffles and put in a saucepan with some water. Boil until just tender, sprinkle with salt and thread on to skewers. Grill lightly. Put the oil, anchovy essence, wine, *caroenum*, honey and pepper in a saucepan and bring to the boil. Add the cornflour mixed with a little water and stir until thickened. Remove the truffles from skewers and serve with the sauce.

'Since, during storms, flames leap from the humid vapours and dark clouds emit deafening noises, is it surprising the lightning, when it strikes the ground, gives rise to truffles, which do not resemble plants?'

Plutarch

LENTILS WITH CHESTNUTS

100 g (4 oz) lentils

100g (4 oz) shelled chestnuts

2.5 ml ($^1/_2$ tsp) bicarbonate
of soda

a pinch of each of the following:
pepper, cumin, coriander seeds,
mint, rue, pennyroyal

1 drop *asafoetida* essence

5 ml (1 tsp) anchovy essence

15 ml (1 tbls) vinegar

15 ml (1 tbls) honey

15 ml (1 tbls) olive oil

Cover the lentils with water and simmer gently for 30 minutes. Put the chestnuts in another pan, cover with water, add bicarbonate of soda and bring to the boil. Cook until tender. Pound the pepper, cumin, coriander seeds, mint, rue and pennyroyal in a mortar. Moisten with *asafoetida* essence, anchovy essence, vinegar and honey, and pour over the cooked chestnuts. Add olive oil and bring to the boil, stirring all the time. Mix with the lentils. Taste and adjust flavouring if necessary. Serve hot.

PURÉE OF LETTUCE LEAVES WITH ONIONS

6 small lettuces
2.5 ml ('/2 tsp) bicarbonate of soda
a pinch of each of the following:
pepper, lovage, celery seeds,
dried mint, oregano
I onion, finely chopped
15 ml (I tbls) wine
15 ml (I tbls) olive oil
5 ml (I tsp) anchovy essence

Plunge the lettuces into a pan of boiling water with the bicarbonate of soda, and simmer for 2 minutes, drain, then chop finely. Pound the pepper, lovage, celery seeds, mint, oregano and onion in a mortar. Add the wine, oil and anchovy essence. Cook gently in a saucepan for 30 minutes, pour over the lettuce, and serve.

STUFFED DATES

6 dates per person
shelled almonds, hazelnuts or
pine kernels (I per date)
pepper
salt
45 ml (3 tbls) honey

Stone the dates and stuff with the nuts and a little pepper. Roll the dates in salt, then heat the honey in a frying pan, fry the dates briskly, and serve.

PATINA OF ELDERBERRIES

6 bunches of elderberries
2.5 ml ($^{1}/_{2}$ tsp) pepper
5 ml (1 tsp) anchovy essence
125 ml (4 fl oz) wine
125 ml (4 fl oz) *passum*
125 ml (4 fl oz) olive oil
6 eggs

Remove the fruits from the stems of the elderberry bunches with a fork. Wash them, place in a saucepan with a little water, and simmer gently until just softened. Drain and arrange in a greased shallow pan. Add the pepper, moisten with anchovy essence, then add the wine and the *passum* and mix well. Finally, add the olive oil and bring to the boil. When the mixture is boiling, break the eggs into it and stir well to bind it together. When set, sprinkle pepper over it and serve hot or cold.

HONEY OMELETTE

4 eggs
275 ml ($^{1}/_{2}$ pt) milk
15 ml (1 tbls) olive oil
45 ml (3 tbls) honey
pepper

Mix together the eggs, milk and oil. Pour a little oil into a frying pan and heat. When it is sizzling, add the prepared mixture. When thoroughly cooked on one side, turn out on a round dish, warm the honey and pour it over the omelette. Sprinkle with pepper and serve.

PEPPERED SWEET CAKE

225 g (8 oz) spelt wheat flour
5 ml (1 tsp) baking powder
2.5 ml (¹/₂ tsp) ground rosemary
100 g (4 oz) almonds, chopped
5 ml (1 tsp) cinnamon
60 ml (4 tbls) sweet sherry
60 ml (4 tbls) grape juice
15 ml (1tbls) honey
milk

To garnish:
filberts or hazelnuts

Mix the flour and baking powder.
Blend with rosemary, almonds and
cinnamon. Combine the wine, grape
juice and honey in a jug. Mix with the
dry ingredients, adding enough milk to
make a soft dropping consistency.
Bake in a 25 cm (9 in) tin at gas
mark 5, 190°C (375°F) for approximately
30 minutes.

For a richer cake, spread the cooked
cake with liquid honey and decorate
with the nuts. Prick the surface with a
fork and drizzle a few tablespoons of
wine into the cake.

When this cake became stale the
Romans soaked it in milk and
fried it in olive oil. It was then
served with yet more honey.

SWEET WINE CAKES

450 g (1 lb) self-raising flour
15 ml (1 tbls) sweet white wine
a pinch of aniseed
a pinch of cumin
50 g (2 oz) lard
25 g (1 oz) cheese, grated
1 egg, beaten
12 bay leaves

Moisten the flour with the wine and add the aniseed and cumin. Rub in the lard and grated cheese and bind the mixture with the egg. Shape into 12 small cakes and place each one on a bay leaf. Bake in the oven at gas mark 6, 200°C (400°F) for about 25–30 minutes.

HONEY CAKES

12 stale sweet wine cakes (see previous recipe)
575 ml (1 pt) milk
45 ml (3 tbls) honey
pepper

Remove the crust from the cakes and steep them in milk. When they are saturated, put them in the oven at gas mark 4, 180°C (350°F) for about 20 minutes. Warm the honey and pour it over the hot cakes, pricking them to absorb more honey. Sprinkle with pepper and serve.

The emblems of a baker's trade displayed on a Roman stone relief of the 2nd century

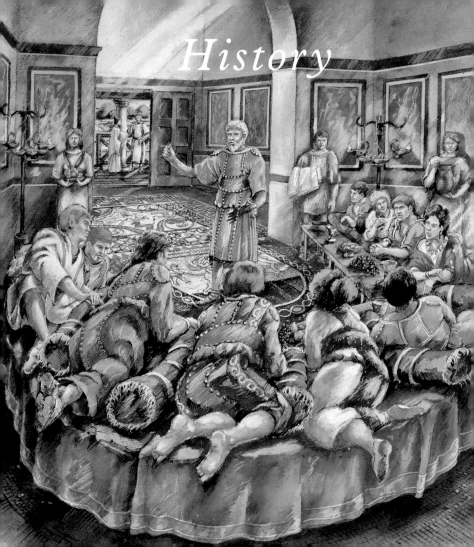

History

ROMAN BANQUETS

Perhaps the best introduction to Roman cooking is to look at the descriptions of some of the most elaborate banquets recorded – bearing in mind that they are exceptions rather than the rule – as they give a vivid insight into the extravagant aspirations and achievements of the Roman cooks. The Romans often sacrificed their culinary skills to the presentation, ostentation and settings of their banquets. At one meal, Heliogabalus served his guest with 600 ostrich brains; peas mixed with grains of gold; lentils with precious stones; and other dishes mixed with pearls and amber – which may have satisfied the guests in some senses, but hardly gastronomically.

The dining room in which the Romans took their meals was known as the *triclinium*, so called because it was usual to arrange three couches around a central dining table, leaving the fourth side open for the serving slaves. Usually three people reclined on each couch to take their meal, with their left arm supported on a cushion. The guests brought their own napkins. Slaves removed the guests' shoes and replaced them with sandals. They performed their ablutions

Opposite: A banquet at the Roman villa at Lullingstone in Kent drawn by Peter Dunn

after each course. When eating they wore a fine napkin around their necks and had another beside them to wipe their fingers.

After invoking Penates, Lares and Jupiter, the feast began. It was usually in three parts. The first course was an hors d'oeuvre. The second was the *coena* or meal proper, after which sacrifices were made to the Lares in great solemnity – the pieces reserved for this were taken to the fire, as was the ancient custom, and a slave offered an oblation to propitious gods from a special goblet. The third course was a dessert which usually consisted of fresh or dried fruit, or fruit in pastries, or honey cakes. Sometimes guests would pick off rose petals and drop them in the wine. Musicians, dancers, acrobats and clowns, and even gladiators, might appear at important feasts to entertain the guests between courses. The combination of rich surroundings, sumptuous and inventive cooking and dazzling entertainment gave the Roman banquets a magnificence seldom achieved since.

Undoubtedly Trimalchio's feast, described by Petronius, was quite exceptional even among the great banquets of imperial Rome, but it is worth recalling in outline here for the atmosphere it conveys. The first course was, as usual, an hors d'oeuvre. A

Cleopatra, the queen of Egypt, gave a 'Pearl Banquet' which was attended by Mark Antony. According to legend she had wagered him that she could give the most expensive banquet of all time. During the feast, she took one of her fabulous pearl earrings, dissolved it in a glass of wine and then drank it. Pearls were highly valued by the Romans and this gesture apparently won the bet.

Corinthian bronze statuette of a horse carrying twin baskets, one filled with black olives, the other with green, was brought in on a tray of relishes. On the back of the animal were two silver dishes with Trimalchio's name engraved on the rim, together with the weight of the metal. Salvers moulded like bridges contained dormice seasoned with poppy seeds and honey. There were also sizzling sausages placed on a silver gridiron with Syrian plums and pomegranate seeds placed beneath it. A tray was placed on the table containing a basket in which sat a carved wooden hen, as if sitting on a nest. Two slaves then revealed that the nest was filled

The Romans added lead pellets to sharp, rough wine to sweeten it. This dangerous practice inevitably caused lead poisoning in some cases.

with pea-fowl eggs, and distributed them to the guests. On breaking them, they were found to be made of light pastry and inside were deliciously spiced garden warblers hidden within the yolks.

Crystal flagons, still sealed and bearing labels inscribed 'Falernian Opimian Wine 100 years old' were then brought in, opened and their contents served to the guests. Whilst they were drinking, a slave put a perfectly made silver model of a skeleton on the table, and demonstrated how the joints and backbone could be articulated in all directions by working a series of springs.

The guests were not quite sure what to make of the second course when it first arrived. It was served on a globe-shaped tray with twelve signs of the Zodiac reproduced on its rim in a circle. Above each sign the chef had placed dishes which, in their shape or nature, had some analogy with the particular constellation: over Aries the Ram there were chickpeas; over Taurus the Bull a piece of beef; over Gemini the Twins kidneys and testicles; over Cancer the Crab a simple crown; over Leo the Lion African figs; over Virgo the Virgin the uterus of a sow; over Libra the Scales a pair of scales with a pie on one side and a cake on the other; over Scorpio the Scorpion a small sea fish; over Sagittarius the Archer a hare; over Capricorn the Goat a lobster; over Aquarius the Water-bearer a goose and over Pisces the Fish two mullets.

In the middle of this contraption was a honeycomb sitting on an artistically cut piece of turf. An Egyptian slave served hot bread to everyone from a silver dish. As the guests were enthusiastically preparing to taste this fare Trimalchio said, 'Let us eat, believe me you have the most succulent of meals before you.'

As he spoke, four slaves removed the top of the globe-shaped table to reveal plump chickens, sows' udders, a hare with wings fastened to its back symbolising Pegasus. At the corners of the tray were four figures of

The winged Pegasus depicted on a mosaic floor at Lullingstone

Marsyas with highly seasoned fish sauce dripping from their bellies over the fish, which were floating about as if they were in a regular canal. The slaves spread covers embroidered with hunting scenes over the couches. Suddenly, there was a loud roar and Laconian hounds burst into the room and began to run round the table followed by an enormous platter on which lay a wild boar, two baskets lined with palm-leaves hanging from its tusks – one filled with Syrian dates and the other with Theban dates. Little sucking pigs made out of pastry were offered to the

Fragment of a 2nd-century Roman pavement from Carthage showing elaborate preparations for a banquet

guests who were allowed to take them away. Drawing his hunting knife, a slave gave the wild boar a great stab in the belly and suddenly out of the opening flew a number of thrushes. They tried in vain to fly out of the room, but were caught in nets and offered to the guests.

When the table had been cleared, three pigs, muzzled and hung with small bells, were driven in, and the host asked his guests which they would like to eat. He then ordered the oldest to be slaughtered. Then the guests were offered more wine grown in his own vineyard.

An enormous pig was served up which covered most of the table, and the guests were amazed at the speed of the cook. Trimalchio examined it, summoned the cook and declared that the pig had not been gutted before cooking. He made as if to have the cook beaten, but then asked the cook to gut it on the spot. When the stomach of the pig was slashed open, out poured black puddings and sausages with which it had been stuffed. The cook was given the privilege of drinking with them and received a silver crown. It certainly seems that to enjoy a Roman feast one had to have a sound constitution.

THE FOODS EATEN IN
ROMAN BRITAIN

There can be no doubt that shellfish were highly prized as food in Roman Britain. Oysters were especially important and may well have been transported live in tanks to inland sites. Oysters from the coast near Colchester and near Richborough were famous and even valued in Rome. The consumption of oysters was so great that the proximity of Roman sites is almost always shown by the presence of large quantities of oyster shells. In one deposit in Silchester more than a million oyster shells were recovered. Other shellfish were also valued for food: periwinkles, mussels, whelks, cockles and scallops have been found on Roman sites. It appears that both at Caerwent and Silchester shellfish shops may have been situated in the east wing of the forum.

Sea fish were also popular: cod, ling, haddock, grey mullet, herring and sea bream were caught, probably with a line and barbed bronze hooks which have also been found. Crabs and lobsters were taken inshore. Whale bones found at Caerwent may indicate that the occasional stranded whale was also fully used for its food potential.

The most characteristic of all ingredients used in Roman cooking was *liquamen* or *garum*. It was made in many different parts of the Empire: several towns were specially renowned for their *liquamen* factories, especially Pompeii and Leptis Magna.

The general effect of these mixtures is something resembling anchovy essence.

The Romans were probably the first people to have the idea of enclosing tracts of land as game parks. In these they kept and hunted red, roe and fallow deer, wild boar and the bears that lived in the remoter parts of Wales and Scotland. Martial describes how some British bears were taken to Rome to take part in wild beast shows. Hunting scenes are depicted on Castor ware pottery made in the Nene Valley which show running figures of dogs, hares and deer in low relief. Game was eaten either roasted or boiled and served with highly flavoured sauces. Venison sauces sometimes include dates in Apicius's recipes.

Not only were large game kept in parks, small game such as hares were kept in *leporia* or hare gardens attached to the villas of the more well-to-do Romans so that they would be quickly available when needed for the table.

'This so called *liquamen* is made as follows: the entrails of fish are thrown into a vessel and salted. Take small fish either atherinae or red mullet or sprats or anchovy and salt all together, and leave out in the sun, shaking it frequently. When it has become dry from heat extract the *garum* from it as follows: take a fine-meshed basket and place it in the middle of the vessel with the above mentioned fish, and in this way the so-called *liquamen* put through the basket can be taken up. If you wish to use the *garum* at once i.e. not expose it to the sun but boil it – make it in the following manner. Take brine and test its strength by throwing an egg into it to try if it floats: if it sinks the brine does not contain enough salt. Put the fish into the brine in a new earthenware pot, add origan, put it on a good fire till it boils … let it cool and strain it over two or three times until clear, seal and store away. The best *garum* is made by taking the entrails of tunny fish and its gills, juice and blood, and add sufficient salt. Leave it in a vessel for two months at most, then pierce the side of the vessel and the *garum*, called Haimation, will flow out.'

Geoponica XX, chapter 46, 1–6

Even smaller animals were kept in confined spaces. Dormice were kept in close captivity enclosed in pottery vessels and fed upon acorns and chestnuts. They were eaten at banquets after having been stuffed with minced pork and dormice meat, and baked in the oven. So far we have little direct evidence for this practice in Britain, though it was very common in other parts of the Empire.

Snails were another delicacy which was treated with care. The snails had to be kept on land entirely surrounded by water to prevent their escape. They were deliberately fed on milk, wine and spelt wheat. For their final fattening they were kept in jars with air-holes. They were fried in oil and served with *liquamen* mixed with wine. Shells of Roman snails have been found on many Romano-British villa sites, indicating that this was a popular form of food.

Wild fowl were also an important source of food; at Silchester swan, goose, wild duck, teal, widgeon, woodcock, plover, crane and stork appear to have been eaten as food. The larger wild fowl were hung for some days to tenderise them. There was a special sauce

Opposite: The Romans were extremely partial to snails and shellfish and usually cooked them in a dark fish sauce called *liquamen*

for those that were 'high' which was strongly flavoured with pepper, lovage, thyme, dried mint, filbert nuts, Jericho dates, honey, vinegar, wine, *liquamen*, oil, wine must and mustard. The problem of removing the sinews from cranes was tackled by cooking them with their heads outside the water. When cooked, the birds were wrapped in a warm cloth and held tightly whilst the head was pulled off with all the sinews attached so that only the meat and bone remained. Roast barnacle goose, *cherneros*, was described by Pliny as the 'most sumptuous dish known to the Britons'.

The Romans practised intensive rearing of delicate birds in special enclosures. They introduced pheasants, peacocks and guinea fowl into Britain, and they may also have kept partridges in captivity as they did in Italy. Peacock meat was so tough that it could only be made palatable if the bird was killed at least a week in advance. The meat was then was converted into rissoles which were stewed in broth to which a little honey and pepper was added after cooking.

Wood pigeons were encouraged to roost in man-made pigeon houses or *columbaria* built in the form of high towers with niches inside where the birds could nest and breed. People living in towns may have had earthenware dovecotes built on the rooftiles of their houses as in the Mediterranean area today. Pigeons can play an important part in supplying meat, and are especially handy if they live in pigeon houses close by.

We have little evidence for the kinds of freshwater fish which were caught, but at Silchester eel, dace, perch, pike and carp are reported, together with bronze fish hooks and the remains of frogs which may have also been eaten.

Salt was obtained from brine by boiling it in an evaporating furnace. Remains of this activity have been identified at Goldhanger, Dymchurch, and Cooling, Kent; Canewdon, Essex; and in the Fens and on the Lincolnshire coast. Salt springs were probably also used at Droitwich and Middlewich in Cheshire.

The arrival of the Romans brought new farming practices to Britain. In southern England villas

'Trust no one unless you have eaten much salt with him.'

Marcus Tullius Cicero (106-43 BC)

of the Italian type were built and new domestic animals were introduced. The treatises of successful landowners on the Continent were read and noted and the management of livestock became much more scientific. The main object was to secure a better supply of meat, though milk, dairy products, hides and wool were also important. The new farming methods included the improved feeding of livestock, and turnips made a significant contribution to the winter fodder.

British cattle were exported to the Continent even before the Romans arrived. Beef appears to have been the preferred meat of Roman Britain, and was supplied as the meat ration of the Roman garrison. There appears to have been several breeds of cattle represented in bones collected from Roman sites; there was the shorthorn *Bos longifrons*; the larger *Bos taurus*, and an even larger form closely similar in size to the wild white Chillingham cattle. Oxen were also present and were the principal beast of burden. They provided milk, butter and cheese for the diet, also meat and leather, bone and horn and glue. Most of the cattle on the military sites in the north of England were of the shorthorn type. The animals represented are usually mature (although some young cattle were present at Newstead) and often their bones had been split for the extraction of the marrow. In one place at Silchester a deposit of 2,500 lower jaws of cattle was discovered, and at another place on the same site 60 cattle horn cores were found – both deposits may be the refuse from some industrial activities but they do show that cattle were available in quite large numbers. At Cirencester, the find below a shop floor of pits filled with cut and sawn bones has suggested that it was in fact a butcher's shop. At the Roman villa at Bignor, Sussex, there were stalls for 55 head of cattle, and a byre for 12 yoke of oxen.

When beef or veal was cooked, it was often sliced and then

Opposite: A reconstruction drawing by Judith Dobie of a butcher's shop

served up in an elaborate sauce. Fried veal was given a sweet and sour sauce composed of raisins, honey, vinegar, pepper, dried onions and herbs.

Pigs were also plentiful, especially in the south and east of the country. Pork was prized by the Roman soldiers and lard was part of their daily rations. The farmers introduced the practice of keeping pigs in sties to fatten them up. Pig sties have been found on two villa sites – Pitney, Somerset and Woolaston Pill, Gloucestershire.

Sucking pig was roasted in the oven and then served with a thickened sauce flavoured with pepper, lovage, caraway, celery seeds, *asafoetida* root, rue, *liquamen*, wine must and olive oil. Sow's udder was put in a mixed *patina* with fish, chicken meat and small birds.

Hams and bacons were either dry salted or pickled in their own brine. Ham and shoulder bacon were recognised as two different meats. According to Apicius, they were both first boiled with dried figs; then the ham was baked in a flour and oil paste, while the bacon was ready to be served with a wine and pepper sauce. An early Roman grave at Grange Road, Winchester in

Hampshire contained a shale tray with a meal set out on it. There were two joints of pork, a Samian ware cup and platter, two knives and a spoon.

The soldiers on Hadrian's Wall and on the Antonine Wall also consumed a fair amount of mutton – large quantities of sheep bones were found at Corbridge and at Barr Hill. The Romano-British sheep seem to have been of light build, somewhat resembling the Soay sheep of St Kilda of today. Sheep pens for 197 sheep have been found at Bignor Roman villa together with what appears to be a lambing enclosure.

Two varieties of goats were also kept, probably as much for their milk as their meat. It may have been the practice to kill and salt the meat of unfit animals for human food.

There is some evidence that horse meat was eaten, possibly in the form of sauces. At Verulamium there is a deposit of aged horse bones which have been dismembered and stripped of their flesh.

Among the remains of birds, those of domestic fowl predominate. They were apparently two varieties: one with small leg bones displaying the well-developed spur of the game cock resembled the modern bantam; the other was the ordinary domestic hen. They are found throughout Roman Britain. The other domestic bird was the goose, probably a variety of the grey lag goose. Boiled or roasted they were served with thick sauces, and they were often given elaborately spiced stuffings. Both birds produced a steady supply of eggs which were also used in cooking.

It seems likely that butter was used in cooking, but there is no evidence for it. The Romans were more accustomed to cooking with olive oil, or lard.

The chief milk product known to be used was cheese. Pottery cheese strainers have been found on many Romano-British sites. Cream cheeses may have been made in the shallow bowls known as *mortaria*. Milk could be left in such bowls to curdle, the whey then being poured off through a spout in the rim. The grits on the inner surface of the bowl would retain the curd-forming bacteria from one cheese-making day to the next, thus obviating the need to use rennet, herbs or old whey to set the milk working. Curd cheeses were flavoured with herbs.

Cheese may have been eaten by itself with bread, but it could also be incorporated in other dishes. Hard cheeses were sometimes

Opposite: A mortaria *and other earthenware vessels of the type used in Roman cooking*

sliced into salads. Softer curd cheeses were used in *patina* dishes mixed with other meat or fish ingredients, hard-boiled eggs, nuts and seasonings.

Honey was a popular flavouring. Columella and Palladius describe how wild swarms of bees are to be trapped in empty hives placed near the observed watering places of bees. The colonies are then installed on hives on the farm. Hives were usually made from wood or withies.

Various forms of wheat were cultivated in Roman Britain. The old hulled varieties of emmer and einkorn continued to be grown but now increasing amounts of spelt wheat was cultivated – probably to meet the corn tax or *annona*. All these hulled wheats need special drying treatment to release their grains efficiently in threshing and it may be for this purpose that the considerable number of corn-drying kilns were erected especially on villa sites, so that the spikelets of hulled wheat could be parched before threshing and grinding.

The naked forms of wheat, bread and club wheat, are also known from Roman Britain but in much smaller quantities. They are much easier to process and gave rise to the varieties of wheat which are cultivated today.

Both the naked and hulled varieties of six-row barley were grown too, but to a smaller extent and it seems that barley was used as punishment rations for soldiers on Hadrian's Wall, and for fodder for horses. Barley may also have been used for brewing.

Sprouted grains of wheat and rye were found together at Carleon in a situation which strongly suggests that they were deliberately sprouted to make malt. The manufacture of beer consists of two processes: malting and fermentation. In the first, the starch in the grain is converted to sugar by the release of the enzyme diastase during the natural germination process. This is encouraged by spreading the grain thinly over a warm floor and giving it a circulation of air and moisture. When the sprouts reached the length of the grain (after a few days), the germination is stopped by giving the malt a mild roasting. The next stage is to steep the malt in water, then to boil it with herbs to give flavour. The fermentation takes place when yeast is added to the wort. The liquid is then drawn off and stored in tightly sealed bottles or barrels.

Possible bases of brewing vats have been found at Silchester where they have been described as 'round furnaces'. In a barn at the Wilcote villa in Oxfordshire, there was a similar round furnace with a flue in which the remains of a brewing vat were found. It was situated near a granary.

Cereal grains were used for baking and for making porridge and gruel. Flour was normally ground at home on rotary hand querns, but there were also some commercial bakers who appear to have used larger hour-glass shaped querns which were driven by donkeys. On Hadrian's Wall, water-driven mills have also been found.

There appears to have been a baker's shop at Canterbury, and at Verulamium an iron slice for removing loaves from the oven probably belonged to another bakery. The Romans made a number of different kinds of bread: *autopyron* was a coarse, dark mixture of bran with a little flour made for the consumption of slaves and dogs; *athletae* was a bread mixed with soft curd cheese, but otherwise unleavened; *buccellatum* was a biscuit or dried bread given to the troops; and *artophites* was a light leavened bread made from the best wheaten flour, and baked in a mould. It was loaves of this sort of bread which were found carbonised in Modestus's ovens at Pompeii.

For a long time the chief Roman food was a kind of gruel made from cereal called *puls* or *pulmentus* which was prepared from barley or spelt wheat which was roasted, pounded and cooked with water in a cauldron to make a porridge similar to modern polenta.

They also made a wheat starch product called *amulum* which was used by Roman cooks for thickening sauces in the same way that we use cornflour today. It was prepared by soaking wheat

Fresh bread made to a Roman recipe

'The cabbage surpasses all other vegetables. If, at a banquet, you wish to dine a lot and enjoy your dinner, then eat as much cabbage as you wish, seasoned with vinegar, before dinner, and likewise after dinner eat some half-dozen leaves. It will make you feel as if you had not eaten, and you can drink as much as you like.'

Cato (Marcus Porcius) (234-149 BC)

grains in fresh water in wooden tubs, and then straining the liquid through linen or wicker baskets before the grain turned sour. The liquid was poured on to a tiled floor spread with leaven, and left to thicken in the sun.

The Romans were enthusiastic about vegetables. They grew peas and beans and imported lentils into Britain. They introduced a number of vegetable crops such as cabbage, onion, leek, carrots, endive, globe artichokes, cucumber, marrow, asparagus, parsnip, radish and celery. They also ate a number of wild vegetable plants including nettles and pennycress.

Herbs were also extensively used in the Roman cuisine and many new ones were introduced to Britain at this time to supplement the poppy seeds, mustard and coriander already known in prehistoric times. The new herbs include aniseed, borage, dill, fennel, garlic, lovage, mint, parsley, rosemary, rue, sage, savory, sweet marjoram and thyme. The Romans much preferred to have their meat flavoured with herbs, either in stuffings or in sauces. A shop selling herb seeds at Colchester was burnt down during Boudicca's rebellion, and the burnt seeds which survived include dill, coriander, aniseed, celery seed and poppy seed.

Sage and rosemary were just two of the many herbs introduced into the British diet by the Romans. They were used lavishly in recipes of the period

'I don't season a dinner the way other cooks do, who serve you up whole pickled meadows in their *patina* – men who make cows their mess mates, who thrust herbs at you then proceed to season those herbs with other herbs. They put in coriander, fennel, garlic and horse parsley, they serve up sorrel, cabbage, beet and spinach, pouring into this a pound of *asafoetida* and pounding up wicked mustard which makes the pounders' eyes water before they've finished. When they season their dinners they don't use condiments but screech owls, which eat out the intestines of the guests alive. That is why life is so short for men in this world, since they stuff their bellies with such like herbs, fearful to speak of, not just to eat. Men will eat herbs which the cows leave alone.'

Plautus

Salads, cooked vegetables, fungi and some light egg or fish dish supplied the hors-d'oeuvre of a Roman meal. Salads were served with a dressing of *liquamen* or *oenogarum* (*liquamen* mixed with wine).

Probably the most important fruit which the Romans introduced into Britain was the grape. Britain lies at the northernmost limit for the ripening of grapes in Europe, and their cultivation was restricted to the southern part of England. Direct evidence for the cultivation of vines comes from the finds of Sir John Evans in 1851 at Boxmoor villa in Hertfordshire. Here he found part of a vineyard with the vinestocks in position. Grape pips have been found widely on Roman sites and at Gloucester they were found together with grape skins and are thought to represent the debris from winemaking.

The local wine was supplemented by imports of considerable quantities of wine-filled amphorae first from Spain and then from south-west France. Wine appears to have been imported in wooden barrels from this area to Silchester. The barrels that survived appear to have been made of silver fir, native to the Pyrenees. Wine was also imported from the Moselle region. The usual drink for soldiers on the Wall was sour or ordinary wine.

Wine intended for use in cooking was reduced by boiling before it was stored. This concentrated its sugars and made it keep better. The boiled-down must or *defructum* was also added to sharp new wines to help them keep.

Wine merchants' shops have been identified at Verulamium, York and Lincoln, usually by the presence of a large number of broken amphorae.

'Vinegar, the son of wine.'

Anon

Grapes may also have been imported in the form of raisins, sultanas or currants, sun-dried in the Mediterranean region.

Vinegar was a very important product. It was manufactured from wine which had gone flat, or had been attacked by the vinegar bacteria during fermentation with additional yeast, salt and honey. Vinegar sharpened sauces and dressings, and was much used in the preservation of fruits, vegetables and even fish. Raw oysters were said to keep well if washed in it, as were pieces of fried fish if plunged into vinegar immediately after cooking. Diluted with several times its volume of water, vinegar made a refreshing drink, and was included in the rations for soldiers on the march. It is possible that the beer-based alegar was also coming into use in Roman times.

The fig is another Roman introduction and may well have been grown in southern England but, because the fruits which ripen here are parthenocarpic and bear their fruit without pollination, they do not develop hard seeds. This means that figs identified by the presence of their seeds alone must come from fruits which have been fertilised through the action of the

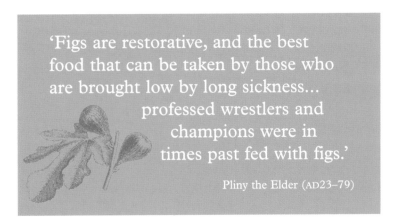

'Figs are restorative, and the best food that can be taken by those who are brought low by long sickness... professed wrestlers and champions were in times past fed with figs.'

Pliny the Elder (AD23–79)

The walnut was associated with Juno, the Roman goddess of women and marriage. This led to the practice of throwing walnuts at a newly married couple as a symbol of fertility.

blastophaga wasp, and have been imported to Britain from warmer climates.

Among the other orchard crops introduced at this time are the medlar, mulberry, damson, plum and cultivated cherry. Apples and pears were also being grown in orchards. Dates found at Colchester and olives from London would have been imported.

Various nut-bearing trees were introduced at this time including the walnut, almond and stone pine. The cones and kernels of the latter seem to have had a ritual as well as culinary significance.

There is ample evidence that the local wild fruits were used in season. Seeds of blackberry, raspberry, strawberry, crab apple, bullace and elder have been found at Silchester.

TECHNIQUES FOR FOOD PREPARATION

Corn-drying kilns were mainly found in association with villas – for example, at Hambledon, Buckinghamshire, where there were at least eight corn-drying kilns (but curiously no granaries for storing it). These kilns are thought to have been used for drying and parching the hulled wheats to make it easier to thresh. They could also have served as suitable places to sprout grain to make malt for brewing. During the 3rd and 4th centuries they occur in increasing numbers, sometimes inserted into the main house as at Brading on the Isle of Wight.

The standard plans of Roman forts include two *horrea* or granaries. These are always buttressed and have raised floors to keep their contents dry. They often have a loading platform at one end. South Shields, which served as a supply base, contains no less than twenty-two granaries. The best preserved examples are at Corbridge and show ventilation slits between the buttresses. The most likely internal arrangement was a central aisle lined with rows of bins.

Opposite: Preparing stuffed kidneys for roasting

A unusual *modius*, an official corn measure, which was found at Carvoran on Hadrian's Wall

Grain storage is always a tricky business and it appears that the granaries at York were subject to infestations of grain weevils. The contents had to be burnt to eradicate this menace.

One unusual find at Carvoran on Hadrian's Wall is of a *modius* or dry measure for grain. It is made of bronze in the shape of a truncated cone about 20 cm (8 in) high. Its capacity of 11.337 litres (2.494 gallons) is unexpected since it exceeds the standard measure of a *modius* by about 10 per cent. One suggestion is that this was a device to defraud provincials who were obliged to deliver a certain amount of wheat. However, Roman certified measures are usually quite accurate and it is possible that the gauge, set lower than the rim, is missing.

The querns of Roman Britain were rotary. The army imported a large number of them from the Rhineland made of Andernach lava. The lower stone was fixed in position and its slightly convex upper surface fitted snugly into the inversely coned lower surface of the upper stone. The upper stone revolved round its axis by means of a wooden or metal handle. Some of these querns are thought to have been ossilatory, the movement of the upper stone being only a quarter turn rather than the normal full rotation.

A larger type of mill, rarely found in Britain, but common at Pompeii has a bi-conical or hour-glass shaped upper stone which revolves round a steeply conical lower stone by means of a heavy wooden lever to which a donkey or mule was sometimes attached. One example of such a mill, made of Andernach lava, was found at Princes Street in London, and another is known from Canterbury. At Silchester, flour appears to have been mainly ground at home, but one establishment seems to have been devoted to grinding flour on a commercial scale. A large hall contained a series of masonry platforms running parallel to the long walls and about 1.5 m (5 ft) away from the nearest one. These seem likely to have been bases for large querns of the hour-glass type.

Reconstruction of an hour-glass shaped quern for grinding corn

COOKING EQUIPMENT

The complex Roman recipes required more careful cooking than the simpler stews, roasts and pottages of the preceding prehistoric cooking tradition. It is therefore not surprising to find that the Romans used more sophisticated cooking equipment. Much of the Roman cooking was done on a raised brick hearth, on top of which was a charcoal fire above which cooking vessels stood on tripods or gridirons. Meat and fish could be directly grilled over burning charcoal on the gridiron. It is possible that wood was burnt on the raised hearths too, especially in the case of dishes which Apicius describes as being smoked. Some very ornamental water heaters were discovered at Pompeii which may have been used for keeping food warm, or possibly for cooking by the bain-marie method. For boiling sucking pig in a cauldron it was likely, in country kitchens at any rate, that it was suspended by chains from the rafters over a more conventional open fire. Wild boar and other large animals were also roasted on spits over wood fires.

Opposite: Step back in time at the Museum of London where a complete Roman kitchen has been recreated

Ovens were used for baking and roasting. They were constructed of rubble and tiles, shaped like low beehives, and provided with a flue to give a draught. Wood or charcoal fires were then lit inside them, the ashes were raked out as soon as the required temperature was reached, the food was put in and the opening of the oven covered to retain the heat. There were also a range of portable ovens (*clibanus*) made of earthenware or iron. They were used for baking bread or keeping dishes warm. Literary sources indicate that they had a rounded vault, wider at the base than at the top, with double walls. A charcoal fire must have been made under the inner floor, the heat percolating between the walls and the fumes escaping through small holes in the outer wall.

Built ovens have been recorded from a number of different sites: at Cirencester a row of 4th-century shops were all equipped with ovens and may have been bakeries. They are a feature on many villa sites and good examples occur at Great Witcombe and Chedworth in Gloucestershire. They have also been found on military sites, sometimes backing on to the ramparts as at Carleon.

Meat was cooked by roasting over a low fire, either on a gridiron or in a portable oven. The latter was suitable for roast neck of mutton, sucking kid or lamb, kidneys and stuffed dormice. Larger joints were either cooked in a baker's oven or grilled on spits over an open fire.

Meat was also stewed in an iron cauldron suspended over an open hearth. Sometimes animals such as stuffed sucking pig were suspended in a basket within a

Kidneys sizzling on a gridiron

cauldron while cooking. Metal vessels became much more widespread and small cauldrons were mass-produced and thus became cheaply available.

A hoard of bronze cooking vessels together with a gridiron were found at the legionary fortress at Newstead. All the pans show signs of hard wear and some are even repaired with bronze patches soldered into place. More frequently cooking pots were used and because they were cheap and widely available they could be thrown away when they became unfit. Porous clay vessels were almost impossible to clean effectively.

A number of specialised cooking pans have been found. The frying pan (*fretale* or *sartago*) was sometimes equipped with a folding handle so that it could be put inside the portable oven as well as being used for cooking over the gridiron. The *patella* was a round shallow pan with a handle, a little deeper than the frying pan, which was used on the table as well as in the kitchen. The *patina* appears to have been an even deeper vessel and was used for making complex dishes with many ingredients – it was somewhat like a casserole without a lid.

There were two other vessels which featured in the kitchen: *mortaria* and *amphorae*. *Mortaria* were special pottery bowls with roughened inner surfaces and a spout on the rim. They were general purpose mixing bowls with heavy rims for lifting, and were first introduced by the Roman army. Gradually, local potteries began to make them. There are also a number of huge *mortaria*, perhaps for use in

bakeries, which were made in the 2nd century by Verecundus of Soller, Kreis Durren, Germany, and imported into Britain.

Amphorae, or two-handled jars, were used in large quantities by the Romans for transporting and storing wine and oil, and remains of many hundreds of them have been found in Britain. After serving their primary purpose, they were often adapted for other uses – they may be set in the floor to store water, and they were even used as coffins. They varied in shape from the early carrot-shaped type with small handles to *amphorae* with long necks and elongated handles, still keeping their pointed bases, and globular forms with short necks and smaller handles. In general it seems that the tall *amphorae* came from France and contained wine, while the globular *amphorae* came from Spain full of precious olive oil.

SERVING THE FOOD

The Romans ate a good deal of their food with their fingers, hence their use of napkins. However, they did have cutlery in the form of knives and spoons – but no forks. Knives were made in all sizes and are frequently found, usually with iron or bronze blades and bronze, wood or bone handles. Spoons were used for eating soft foods and sauces. They are also found quite frequently and are made from silver, bronze or bone and have either round or oval bowls. A small spoon known as a *cocleare* was used at the bowl end for eating eggs and the pointed handle end for picking shellfish out of their shells. The round-bowled spoons are earlier, whereas the lyre-shaped, oval bowl forms predominated in the 3rd and 4th centuries. Larger spoons and ladles of bronze or iron may have been used for serving up food.

Opposite: A variety of copper cooking utensils

Right: Roman spoon mould

Equipment for serving wine was often very elaborate. It was sometimes imported, and includes special strainers with the perforations arranged in patterns, silver jugs, dishes, cups and goblets and enamelled wine ladles, cups and finger bowls.

Dining tables were sometimes equipped with ornate lamps, candelabra and sets of heated dishes. There can be little doubt that the furnishings of the table together with the interior décor of the dining room were the signs by which Romans judged social standing.

The table was also furnished with plates made either of pewter such as those from 4th-century London, or silver (the most exotic known in this country are from the magnificent Mildenhall treasure which were probably intended for show rather than use), or

Opposite: A selection of knives used in Roman cookery

Right: An intricately decorated pewter flagon and handle

from the cheerful, bright red Samian ware. This was imported from France and comes in two forms: large bowls with decoration in relief and a range of smaller bowls and platters which are undecorated.

Glass was much less common than pottery but included bowls, beakers, bottles and jugs usually made of a pale greenish colour. However, examples of white, amber, blue and yellowish green glass are known, and there are a few examples with the late polychrome glass from Roman London.

Two forms of metal jugs are also known to have been made in either pewter or bronze. There is a rather bulky wide-mouthed jug with a broad neck which merges

Above: Glass vessel found at Wall Roman site (Letocetum) in Staffordshire

Left: A large Samian ware bowl from Aldborough Roman Site in Yorkshire

without division into the body; and a relatively narrow-necked form which is much more graceful and has its neck clearly separated from its bulbous body by a line of decoration.

There can be little doubt that the Romans gave a great deal of thought and went to some trouble in order to serve their food as elegantly and imaginatively as possible.

Copper alloy vessels found at Stanwick Quarry, Raunds, Northamptonshire

BIBLIOGRAPHY

Alcock, Joan P., *Food in Roman Britain*, Tempus (Stroud, 2001).

André, J., *L'Alimentation et la cuisine à Rome*, Librairie C. Klincksieck (Paris, 1961).

Flower, B. and Rosenbaum, E. (eds), *The Roman Cookery Book, a critical translation of The Art of Cookery by Apicius*, Harrap (London, 1958; reprinted 1974).

Wilson, C.A., *Food and Drink in Britain*, Constable (London 1973); Penguin Books (Harmondsworth, 1976).

ACKNOWLEDGEMENTS

The publishers would like to thank Shirley Walsh (aka Sosia Juncina) for cooking and presenting a number of recipes in this book. We would also like to thank her for giving us permission to use the recipes on pp 33 and 40 which are taken from her book *Sosia's Kitchen*.

The publishers are grateful for the help given by Dr René Rodgers, Dr John Pearce and Anne Jones (Curator, Museum of Farnham, Surrey) in the preparation of this book.

Many of the photographs which appear in the book were taken by Peter Williams, and the publishers would like to express their appreciation of his superb work.

The publishers would like to thank the following people and organisations listed below for permission to reproduce the photographs in this book. Every care has been taken to trace copyright holders, but any omissions will, if notified, be corrected in any future edition.

All photographs are © English Heritage or © Crown copyright.NMR with the exception of the following: Front cover: The British Museum; p9 Roger-Viollet, Paris/courtesy of The Bridgeman Art Library; p11 Museo Archaeologico Nazionale, Naples/courtesy of The Bridgeman Art Library; pp13,16,52,69,78,85 Derry Brabbs; p43 Roger-Viollet, Paris/courtesy of The Bridgeman Art Library; p50 Louvre, Paris, France/courtesy of The Bridgeman Art Library; p82 Museum of London

Line illustrations by Peter Brears

RECIPE INDEX